What's in the SOUTHWEST?

Lyons Mill Elementary School
Baltimore County Public Schools

By Lynn Peppas

Crabtree Publishing Company
www.crabtreebooks.com

Crabtree Publishing Company

www.crabtreebooks.com

Author: Lynn Peppas
Publishing plan research and development:
    Sean Charlebois, Reagan Miller
    Crabtree Publishing Company
Proofreader: Crystal Sikkens
Editorial director: Kathy Middleton
Photo research: Katherine Berti, Crystal Sikkens
Designer: Ken Wright
Production coordinator: Ken Wright
Prepress technician: Ken Wright
Print coordinator: Katherine Berti

Photographs:
Dreamstime: pages 8 (inset), 26, 29 (bottom)
Wikimedia Commons: Leaflet: page 8 (left); USDA
    Forest Service, Coconino National Forest: page
    13; Cacophony: page 14 (right); cliff1066: page 18
    (right); Eric Guinther: page 21 (left)
Other images by Shutterstock

Illustrations:
Bonna Rouse: pages 14 (left), 15

Cover description: (top left) Austin, Texas' capital city, is home to a large financial district. (center left) Oil is a major natural resource in the Southwest region. (top right) Early pueblo homes can be seen at Bandelier National Monument in New Mexico. (bottom) With close to five million visitors each year, the Grand Canyon is one of the world's leading natural attractions.

Title page description: The Taos Pueblo in New Mexico is estimated to be 1000 years old.

Library and Archives Canada Cataloguing in Publication

Peppas, Lynn
    What's in the Southwest? / Lynn Peppas.

(All around the U.S.)
Includes index.
Issued also in electronic formats.
ISBN 978-0-7787-1826-0 (bound).--ISBN 978-0-7787-1832-1 (pbk.)

    1. Southwestern States--Juvenile literature.
I. Title. II. Series: All around the U.S.

F785.7.P46 2012   j979   C2011-905578-3

Library of Congress Cataloging-in-Publication Data

Peppas, Lynn.
    What's in the Southwest? / Lynn Peppas.
        p. cm. -- (All around the U.S.)
    Includes index.
    ISBN 978-0-7787-1826-0 (reinforced library binding : alk. paper)
    -- ISBN 978-0-7787-1832-1 (pbk. : alk. paper) -- ISBN 978-1-4271-8780-2 (electronic pdf) -- ISBN 978-1-4271-9713-9 (electronic html)
    I. Title. II. Series.

F785.7.P47 2011
979--dc23
                                        2011032237

Crabtree Publishing Company

Printed in Canada/092013/TT20130814

www.crabtreebooks.com   1-800-387-7650

Published in Canada
Crabtree Publishing
616 Welland Ave.
St. Catharines, ON
L2M 5V6

Published in the United States
Crabtree Publishing
PMB 59051
350 Fifth Avenue, 59th Floor
New York, New York 10118

Published in the United Kingdom
Crabtree Publishing
Maritime House
Basin Road North, Hove
BN41 1WR

Published in Australia
Crabtree Publishing
3 Charles Street
Coburg North
VIC 3058

CONTENTS

Words that are defined in the glossary are in **bold** type
the first time they appear in the text.

Welcome to the U.S.A.

The United States of America is the world's third largest country in size and population. It is the middle country in the **continent** of North America. It shares a border with the country of Canada to the north, and Mexico to the south. The United States has two natural water borders. To the east of the United States is the Atlantic Ocean and to the west is the Pacific Ocean. The country is divided into 50 states and one district. Alaska and Hawaii are the only two states that are not located between Canada and Mexico. Alaska borders the northwest of Canada. It is also the largest U.S. state. Hawaii is a group of islands located southwest of the mainland United States in the Pacific Ocean.

What are Regions?

The United States is divided into regions. Regions are areas of land that share common features or characteristics with one another. The United States is so large that one region can be very different from another. For example, an American living in Alaska lives in a very different area than an American living in Arizona.

U.S. Capital

Washington is the capital of the United States. It is located in a special part of the country called the District of Columbia.

Why are Regions Needed?

Regions help people describe and understand an area. A region can be as small as a neighborhood, or as big as a group of states. Regions describe areas that share characteristics such as politics, wildlife, economy, landforms, climate, and many more.

The Five U.S. Regions

In this series, the United States is divided into five different regions. These regions are called the Northeast, Southeast, Midwest, Southwest, and West. They are created from states that are close together. The states in a region share common characteristics such as landforms, climate, history, economy, and culture. This book explores the common features of the states that make up the Southwest region.

The Southwest Region

Of the five regions, the Southwest has the smallest number of states—just four. This does not mean it is the smallest region though. The states included in the Southwest are Arizona, New Mexico, Texas, and Oklahoma. In terms of area Texas is the second largest U.S. state, with New Mexico coming in fifth largest, and Arizona being the sixth largest. The number of states in this region might be small, but they cover a big area!

Austin is the capital city of Texas and home to close to 800,000 people.

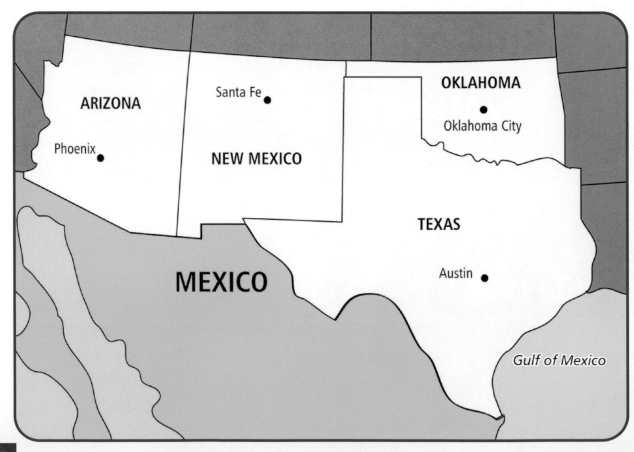

Southwest Borders

Three southwestern states, Arizona, New Mexico, and Texas, share a border with the country of Mexico. The Southwest has only one natural water border—the Gulf of Mexico. It is located on the southeast border of Texas.

Americans choose to make the Southwest region their home because of the rich culture and beautiful landscapes. Many senior-aged Americans choose to retire in the area because of the warm, year-round climate. Texas is the second-largest state by population in the United States. With so many living in the region it only makes sense that four of the top ten most populous cities can be found in the Southwest region. These densely populated cities, in order of population, are Houston, Texas, Phoenix, Arizona, San Antonio, Texas, and Dallas, Texas.

Four Corners

The Four Corners is the only place in the United States where four states meet at one single point. Two states in the Southwest region, Arizona and New Mexico, make up the bottom half of the "four corner" region.

Utah and Colorado join Arizona and New Mexico to make up the Four Corners. A marker stands at the point where these four states meet.

Landforms

The Southwest region has a wide variety of landforms. Landforms are the natural surfaces that occur on Earth. The Southwest region is known for its wondrous canyons, **plateaus**, and starkly beautiful desert landscapes.

Highs and Lows of the Southwest

The Great Plains is a broad area of flat land that runs throughout the Southwest and Midwest region. Most of Texas and Oklahoma are covered by the Great Plains. The High Plains is a sub-region of the Great Plains that rises in height from about 1,100 feet (335 m) to over 7,800 feet (2,377 m).

It lies in the western part of both states and stretches into New Mexico. This area has deep and broad valleys cut in the rock by rivers. West of the Great Plains, in central New Mexico, the land rises up into the Rocky Mountain range. The highest point in New Mexico is Wheeler Peak with an elevation of over 13,000 feet (3,962 m). There are other mountain ranges in New Mexico such as the Guadalupe, Mogollon, Organ, Sacramento, and San Andres. Between these mountains lie desert basins.

New Mexico has very different landforms from the flat, open High Plains (below) to the rigid cliffs of the Rocky Mountains (inset).

Colorado Plateau

The Colorado Plateau is an area of many elevated plateaus over 5,000 feet (1,524 m). The plateaus are not flat on top, and many are reddish-brown colored rock. Canyons separate the plateaus. In the Southwest region, the Colorado Plateau covers the northwest corner of New Mexico, and the northern part of Arizona. The Grand Canyon is the highest area of the Colorado Plateau.

The Grand Canyon

The Grand Canyon is in northern Arizona. A canyon is a deep, narrow valley with steep rock walls. Some of Earth's oldest rock can be seen at the bottom of the canyon.

Billions of years ago, the rock lifted and folded to create a 6-mile (9.6 km) high mountain range. Over time the mountain range eroded, or was worn down, into a plain. About one billion years ago, the plain folded up once again to form another mountain range. This mountain range eroded over millions of years, too, and was covered by an ancient sea. Over time, the sea bottom rose up once again to form a plateau. The sea drained forming the Colorado River about 17 million years ago. The river's rushing waters have cut into the rock of the plateau to create the Grand Canyon we see today. In the process it unearthed billions of years of geologic history.

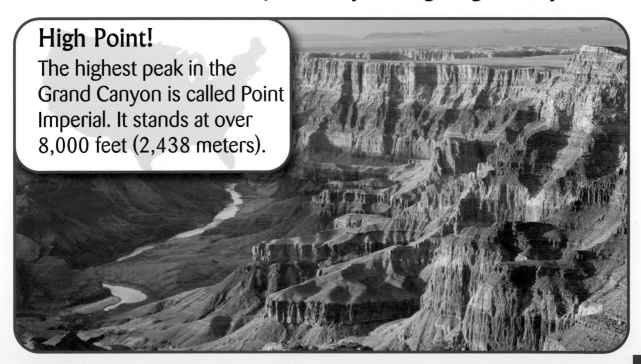

High Point!

The highest peak in the Grand Canyon is called Point Imperial. It stands at over 8,000 feet (2,438 meters).

A Cool Drink of Water

The Southwest is home to a number of water sources such as rivers, aquifers, and the Gulf of Mexico. These water sources that run throughout the region have carved out much of the area's scenery and provide a cool drink of water for the dry, often rocky landscapes in the area.

crab

Gulf of Mexico

The Gulf of Mexico is the southeast border of Texas. Along Texas' shore are wetlands and estuaries. An estuary is a coastal body of water that connects seawater with fresh, inland water from the San Jacinto and Trinity Rivers. Galveston Bay is the largest estuary in Texas. Its ecosystem supports marine life such as crabs, shrimps, and oysters.

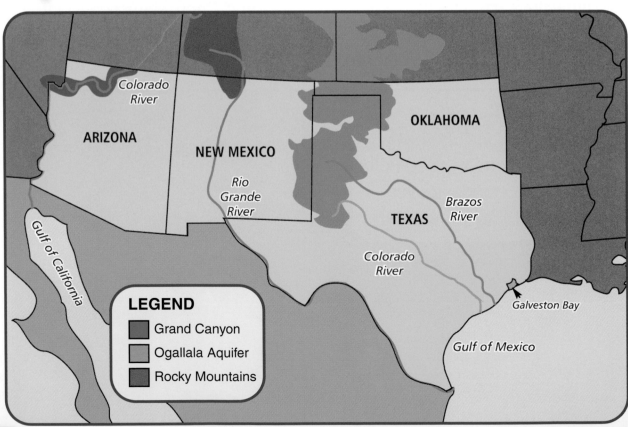

Colorado River

ARIZONA

NEW MEXICO

OKLAHOMA

Rio Grande River

Brazos River

TEXAS

Gulf of California

Colorado River

LEGEND

■ Grand Canyon
□ Ogallala Aquifer
■ Rocky Mountains

Galveston Bay

Gulf of Mexico

Underground Aquifers

An aquifer is an underground area of rock that holds water. Aquifers are fed by **groundwater**. They are also **replenished** by rainwater and melted snow. The Ogallala Aquifer lies in the east of New Mexico, the northwest area of Texas, and the western area of Oklahoma. It holds about the same amount of water as Lake Huron. Water from the aquifer is pumped out for residential, agricultural, and industrial use. The Basin and Range aquifers are found in the southern area of Arizona.

The Rio Grande River starts in the Rocky Mountains and flows to the Gulf of Mexico, making it the fifth longest river in North America.

Rivers Run Through It

Freshwater rivers are the lifeblood of the Southwest. Many of the rivers, such as the Colorado River, beat a path through the Southwest to drain into the Gulf of Mexico or the Gulf of California. The Rio Grande River is a natural border between the United States and Mexico through the state of Texas, and flows into the Gulf of Mexico. Brazos River is the longest river in Texas. It flows through northwest Texas and into the Gulf of Mexico. Other major rivers of the area include the Canadian River, Red River, and Arkansas River.

The Climate

Many people choose to live in the Southwest because of the warm, year-round climate. Climate is the average weather over a period of time. Most of the Southwest region enjoys warm winters and hot summers, especially in the more southern areas. During winters in the high mountain areas people can enjoy snow sports such as downhill skiing.

Texas Flood!

They say things are bigger in Texas, but so are the storms! Texas gets a lot of thunderstorms, tornadoes, and hurricanes. Hurricanes form over the Gulf of Mexico and travel on to the coast of this state.

Extreme Weather

Much of the Southwest has an arid climate. Arid describes an area that is very dry with little precipitation. New Mexico and Arizona have arid climates. Many areas get less than 15 inches (38 cm) of precipitation in a year! The western halves of Texas and Oklahoma have an arid to semi-arid climate. The eastern half of Texas has a **humid**, subtropical climate. The state is so large that there is snowfall in the northern area of the state, but the southern area very rarely gets any snow. Arizona and New Mexico have alpine climates with large amounts of snowfall in the mountain regions.

The Chihuahuan Desert gets less than 10 inches (25 cm) of rain a year.

Deserts

Deserts are dry areas with extreme temperatures. Average daytime temperatures during the summer months range from 95 to 104 degrees Fahrenheit (35-40 degrees Celsius). The Chihuahuan Desert is the largest desert in North America. It is in the southern parts of Arizona, New Mexico, and Texas in the United States and is also in Mexico.

Tornado Alley

Tornadoes are violent, funnel-shaped storms that can be very destructive to everything in its path. Tornado Alley is an area in the center of the United States where tornadoes most often occur. The Southwest states of Texas and Oklahoma are in Tornado Alley. Texas has more tornadoes than any other state in the U.S., and average over 130 tornadoes every year. Oklahoma has fewer but they are considered to be more dangerous. Tornadoes usually occur during the spring and summer. Tornadoes occur in this area because the hot, moist air from the Great Plains rises up and creates thunderstorm clouds. Tornadoes form during thunderstorms when the hot air rises quickly and meets the cooler air and thunderclouds.

Mountains

A mountain climate changes at different altitudes, or heights. Air cools as it rises and temperatures are much colder on the top of a mountain than the base. Mountain areas also affect precipitation. Winds carry warm air masses up a mountain. Warm air holds moisture. As the warm air travels upward the air cools, and drops its precipitation on the mountain. It falls in the form of rain or snow.

The snow on the San Francisco Peaks mountain range in northern Arizona, creates a much different climate than the deserts to the south.

The First Peoples

Thousands of years ago the Southwest was home to different nations of Native Americans. Many of the earliest Native American cultures were farmers who settled in permanent homes. These ancient Native nations are thought to be some of the most advanced cultures in North America.

Ancient Pueblo Peoples

Ancient Pueblo peoples were a nation of Native Americans that lived in the Southwest thousands of years ago. They lived in the northern areas of Arizona and New Mexico. About a thousand years ago, the ancient Pueblo peoples built large homes in the rock walls of canyons from **adobe**. When Spanish explorers came to the Southwest in the 1500s they called these buildings pueblos. The people living in the pueblos became known as the Pueblo peoples. This ancient culture were the ancestors of other Native American nations today such as the Hopi and Zuni.

(above) The remains of one of the ancient Pueblo peoples' settlements can be seen in Arizona at the Canyon de Chelly.

(left) Pueblos were apartment-style homes that held many families. They offered protection from **nomadic** enemy nations such as the Navajo peoples. The thick adobe walled houses also insulated them from the heat.

Apache Native Americans

Native Americans that spoke the Athapascan language **migrated** from present-day western Canada to the Southwest in the 1200s. Zuni Native Americans called them "Apachu," which meant "enemy" in their language. They were nomads, which meant they did not live in permanent villages. They were also known as fierce warriors. Geronimo was a famous Apache chief who fought against American settlers in the 1800s.

Navajo

Navajo Native Americans speak the Athapascan language and are related to the Apache nation. They migrated to the Southwest region from western Canada thousands of years ago. The ancient Pueblo peoples taught them to farm. The Navajo are the largest group of Native Americans in the United States today. A large part of their 16 million acre **reservation** is in Arizona.

Oklahoma Indian Territory

In 1830, the American government forced Native Americans living in the east to move to the west. The journey was difficult and many had to walk thousands of miles (km). It was called the Trail of Tears because many Native Americans died of disease or starvation along the way. The United States government set aside land in Oklahoma for many different Native American nations. Today, Oklahoma is still home to many Native Americans. In fact, Oklahoma means "red person" in the Choctaw language.

(left) The Navajo lived in homes called hogans that were made from logs, bark, and mud.

(right) The Navajo people wore colorful blankets and sashes.

European Settlers

The Spaniards were the first Europeans to discover the Southwest region. They claimed Texas as their colony in the 1500s but the area was much larger than today's state of Texas and included parts of Oklahoma and New Mexico. The Southwest region underwent changes in government during the 1800s and was, at one time, its own country until the United States claimed it as their own in 1845.

New Spain

The first European to ever see the Southwest was a Spanish explorer named Alonso Álvarez de Pineda. He discovered Texas in 1519 while searching for a water route to Asia from the Gulf of Mexico. Spain claimed what is Mexico today and the Southwest region of the United States in the 1500s. They called the area New Spain. Francisco Vasquez de Coronado was a Spanish ruler and explorer. He was the first European to explore modern-day Arizona, New Mexico, Texas, and Oklahoma between 1540–1542.

Mission San José still stands in San Antonio, Texas. San Antonio was the center for missions in Texas.

Spanish Missions

In the 1700s, Spain wanted to expand their influence throughout the Southwest region. They were worried that another country such as Britain, France, or the United States, would take over the area. New Spain paid religious leaders called missionaries to set up missions or colonies of Native Americans living in Texas. These missionaries were the first European settlers in the Southwest region. They taught Native Americans the Christian religion. They wanted Native Americans to forget their heritage and practice **Hispanic** culture and traditions instead.

Breaking From Spain

In 1821, Mexican revolutionaries fought with the Spanish colonials and won the Mexican War of Independence. Spain no longer owned Mexico or the Southwest.

Mexican-American War

In 1836, Texas claimed independence from Mexico and became its own country called the Republic of Texas. The Mexican government refused to recognize their independence.

In 1845, Texas joined the United States when they **annexed** the Southwest region that included modern-day areas of Texas, Oklahoma, Arizona, and New Mexico. Mexico was not in favor of the annexation and in 1846 they declared war on the United States. When the American army captured Mexico City in 1848, the Mexicans agreed to give the Southwest region to the United States for $15 million dollars. That would be worth over $373 million today!

Mexican troops launched an attack on the Alamo Mission near San Antonio, Texas, in 1836. Many Texans were killed trying to defend their mission. The loss of the battle inspired Texans to join the army and they went on to defeat the Mexicans in the Battle of San Jacinto a few months later, claiming their independence. An historical reenactment is held each year at the Alamo to remember the battle and honor the people who were killed.

Population Distribution

The Southwest region has highly populated big cities and surrounding metropolitan areas. In rural, desert areas the population is very low. In 2010, Arizona, New Mexico, and Texas were some of America's fastest growing states in terms of population. The region has a variety of ethnicities but the majority living there are Anglo-American and Hispanic-American peoples.

The First Anglo Settlement
The first Anglo-Americans to settle in the Southwest started coming in 1822 and are called "The Old 300." An American named Stephen F. Austin was the first **empresario** to settle the colony of Americans in Texas. American settlers moved to get free grants of land in Texas near the Brazos River, but they had to become Mexican citizens.

Retirees

Today, many retirees are moving to Southwestern states such as Arizona to enjoy the warm, dry climate. People with breathing ailments find the dry air to be much healthier.

Stephen F. Austin is often called the Father of Texas.

Oklahoma Land Run

The Oklahoma Land Run of 1889 took place on April 22. A land run, or rush, is the instant occupation of land for homesteading. Over two million acres (almost one million hectares) was available for settlement. Cities of up to 10,000 people in Oklahoma, such as Oklahoma City and Guthrie, sprang up in just one day. On April 22, it is estimated that 50,000 people moved to Oklahoma. The land run was to begin at noon but some people entered the area sooner or earlier than others to pick out the best lands. This led to the nickname "Sooner State."

Big Cities

Most of the population in the Southwest tends to live in large cities and surrounding metropolitan areas. The largest city in Arizona is its capital, Phoenix. The city has almost one and a half million people. The surrounding metropolitan area has over four million people. Texas has a number of densely populated cities such as Dallas, Houston, and San Antonio. Houston is the fourth largest city in the United States. Over two million people live there. San Antonio is another large Texas city and is the seventh largest city in the United States.

Phoenix, Arizona, is the sixth most populated city in the United States.

Natural Resources

Natural resources are materials found in nature that can be made into products. The Southwest region is rich in oil and natural gas reserves and agriculture. There is also a wealth of minerals found in this area such as helium, zinc, copper, gold, and silver to name a few! Water is a valuable natural resource in the Southwest because of the dry climate. People from the Southwest conserve water in different ways to make it last a longer time.

Oil pump jack

Oil and Natural Gas

The Southwest region is the leading producer of crude oil. Crude oil is a non-renewable resource from which gasoline, diesel fuel, and other petroleum products such as crayons, CDs and DVDs, and tires are made. It is pumped out of reserves found underground. Texas produced 21% of all crude oil in the United States in 2010. Natural gas is also found in reserves under the ground. It is an invisible, odorless gas. It is used to heat homes and power machines in industries. Oklahoma and Texas are some of the leading producers of natural gas.

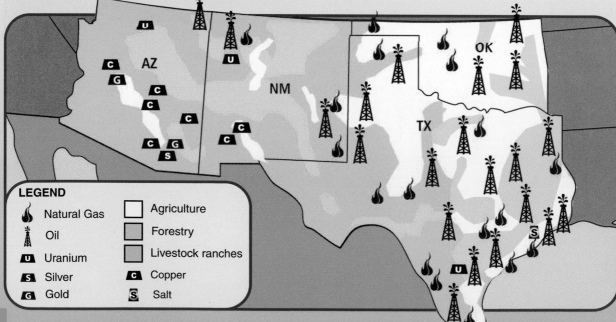

LEGEND

- Natural Gas
- Oil
- U Uranium
- S Silver
- G Gold
- Agriculture
- Forestry
- Livestock ranches
- C Copper
- S Salt

Mining

The Southwest region abounds in valuable minerals. Arizona is the largest producer of copper in the United States. New Mexico is also wealthy in minerals and is the leading producer of uranium ore, salt, and manganese ore.

Agriculture

When it comes to agriculture, Texas is the most important state in the United States. There are more farms in Texas than any other state and it produces more cattle, and cotton than any other state, too. The plains in Oklahoma are a perfect spot for growing wheat, cotton, and raising livestock for beef and pork production. Much of New Mexico is dry, desert land. The land that is suitable for agriculture is used for grass to feed cattle. Arizona crops include cotton, lettuce, and cattle farming.

(above) The primary breed of cattle that started the cattle industry in the Southwest was the Texas longhorn.

(above) Cotton plants grow well in the Southwest climate.

(left) The Chino copper mine was started in 1909. It is located near Silver City, New Mexico, and is possibly the oldest mine still in use in the Southwest.

Water Conservation

All living things such as plants and animals need water to survive. The Southwest is an arid region where water is not as plentiful as other states. For thousands of years people living in the Southwest have had to conserve fresh water sources. Animals and plants have had to adapt to the often hot, dry climate.

Desert Animals

Animals that live in desert climates have to adapt to the hot and dry conditions. Desert Bighorn sheep live in desert mountain and foothill ranges such as those in New Mexico and Texas. They use their horns to remove the outer layer of cacti so they can get water from the insides. Some desert animals such as the Kangaroo rat burrow homes underground to keep cool. The Greater Roadrunner is a bird that conserves its heat during cold desert nights by slowing down its bodily functions. During the day it heats up quickly with a dark patch of skin on its back that attracts and absorbs the heat from the Sun.

Plants

Desert plants have adapted to the dry and hot climate conditions of the Southwest region. Some plants, called xerophytes, have very few or no leaves at all. Some plants have very long roots and get water from underground aquifers. Mesquite trees have very long root systems that draw water from underground. Some root systems have been found to be 80 feet (24 m) deep.

Cacti, such as the Prickly-Pear cactus, have no leaves and shallow root systems. When it does rain they store excess water in their stems.

The Greater Roadrunner is a fast runner, it can run up to 15 mph (24 km/h)!

Irrigation in the Southwest

Agriculture needs a constant supply of water to grow and flourish. Thousands of years ago Native Americans such as the Anasazi built dams and canals that redirected water into their fields. They dug wells to gather underground water. They planted crops using a grid system, which meant a small area would have raised soil borders. This kept any rainwater that fell within the small area, and it would not runoff during heavy rains. Today, farmers in the Southwest still use similar methods but have greatly improved upon them. Farmers pump water from underground aquifers to irrigate crops.

Water Dams

Dams are human-made barriers or walls that stop the flow of water. There are a number of dams in the Southwest region that are used for irrigation, to control flooding, and produce **hydroelectric** power. The Hoover Dam is a concrete dam that was built on the border of Arizona and Nevada. It holds back the Colorado River and has created Lake Mead. It provides a power source for Arizona, California, and Nevada. Other dams in the Southwest region include the Cochiti Dam in New Mexico, the Eufaula Dam in Oklahoma, and the Medina Dam in Texas.

Construction began on the Hoover Dam in 1931 and was completed in 1936. It was the largest dam in the world when it was first built.

Economy

The Southwest region leads the nation in many natural resources such as minerals, oil and natural gas, and agriculture. The region is also an important service industry area with businesses such as private health care centers, and tourism.

Fort Worth Stockyards Station, in Texas, was once a major place to buy and sell cattle. Today, tourists can visit and learn about the history of Stockyards Station and even see a Texas longhorn **cattle drive**.

Manufacturing

Instead of shipping their raw resources elsewhere, the region manufactures most of these natural resources into products and is one of the leading areas for manufacturing. The Southwest manufactures computers and electronic equipment, and chemicals such as fertilizers.

Food Production

The Southwest region leads the nation in cotton and beef cattle production. Texas alone produces 20 percent of the country's beef cattle. Other important crops such as wheat, hay, lettuce, onions, cabbages, and pecans are also farmed in the Southwest. The Southwest processes much of their natural foods into dairy products, baked goods, preserved fruits, vegetables, and meats.

Pecan nuts are grown on trees in most of the Southwest states.

Oil Production

The Southwest is responsible for about 20 percent of the country's oil production, and about 30 percent of the country's natural gas supplies. Texas leads the country in production of mined products, which includes natural gas and oil. Other Southwest states such as New Mexico and Oklahoma are among the leading producers, too. Oil and natural gas are pumped from the ground. It is refined into other products such as gasoline and fuel for jets called kerosene. Natural gas is transported through pipelines to other states throughout the United States. When natural gas is cooled, it changes into a liquid state and can be transported on ships or transport trucks.

There are many oil refineries in Texas, such as this one in Corpus Christi.

Southwest Culture

Ethnic groups are people who share a similar cultural heritage. They, or their relatives, have moved to America from the same country. Ethnic groups have things in common such as religion, language, and appearance. Americans are proud to describe their country as a mosaic or salad bowl that is made up of many different cultures.

Southwest Mosaic

The Southwest region is a mosaic of many different cultures such as Anglo-Americans, Hispanics, African Americans, Asian Americans, and Native Americans. A large population of Hispanic Americans live in the states of Texas, New Mexico, and Arizona, which share a border with the country of Mexico. Many have immigrated from Mexico either recently, or hundreds of years ago when the area was first being settled. Hispanic Americans living in Phoenix, Arizona, make up almost half the population. Many reside in large cities in Texas such as Houston, San Antonio, and Dallas.

Juneteenth

Juneteenth is an American holiday that celebrates freedom from slavery in the United States. Even though freedom for all Americans came into effect when the Civil War ended on April 9, 1865, Americans living in Texas did not hear about it until June 19, 1865. To this day, Americans travel to Texas to take part in special Juneteenth celebrations. Many go to the Booker T. Washington State Park, which is a 30-acre (12-hectare) park in Houston, Texas. People hold outdoor barbecue picnics or attend Juneteenth festivals that teach about African-American history. Some go to concerts and listen to music such as jazz.

Members of the Greater Houston All-Star Band perform in a Juneteenth parade in Houston, Texas.

Native American Festivals

The Southwest enjoys exciting events and festivals that highlight Native American cultures. The largest Native American populations in the United States live in areas of New Mexico and Arizona. The Gathering of Nations is an annual dance competition held in Albuquerque, New Mexico. More than 3,000 dancers from over 500 nations of Native Americans from all over North America including Canada and Mexico compete in this colorful display of traditional costume and dance.

(right) An enchilada is filling wrapped in a tortilla and covered in a chili pepper sauce. (below) People of all ages enjoy the Gathering of Nations annual powwow held on the fourth weekend in April.

Hispanic Heritage Month

In Arizona from September 15 to October 15, people celebrate Hispanic or Latino culture. In Phoenix, events are held throughout the month to celebrate the independence of Hispanic countries such as Mexico, Guatemala, and Costa Rica. Concerts with traditional Latin musicians and dancers perform traditional Hispanic music such as flamenco. Festivals also feature Southwestern Latino foods such as enchiladas and chimichangas.

Places to Visit

The tourism industry in the Southwest attracts millions of people every year. The warm, sunny climate, variety of cultures, national parks, and scenic landscapes draw tourists to the Southwest region from all over the world.

Spectacular Stonework

Visitors come to Arizona to see some of the ancient dwellings in the numerous canyons throughout the state. Montezuma Castle is one of these buildings located in the northern part of Arizona. It is a five-story building with 20 different rooms inside. It was built almost 1,000 years ago by Sinagua Native Americans. Tourists interested in seeing ancient ruins in New Mexico visit the Aztec Ruins National Monument near Aztec, New Mexico. Native Americans built the walled village almost 1,000 years ago. It has about 400 rooms on three levels.

Montezuma castle is one of the best-preserved Pueblo cliff dwellings in the Southwest.

The Grand Canyon

Although it isn't the biggest or deepest canyon in the world, the Grand Canyon is by far one of the most famous attractions in North America. People are awestruck by the sheer size and beauty of the canyon. It is 277 miles (446 km) long, and up to 18 miles (29 km) wide. Tourists can whitewater raft on the Colorado River through the Grand Canyon. Tourists also enjoy hiking and helicopter tours of the canyon.

Cowboy Culture

When people think of Texas they imagine the days of the Wild West and cowboys. Rural areas of Texas still feature ranches and rodeos that tourists can watch or tour. Events that tourists enjoy are horse shows, county fairs, and rodeos.

Powwows

Oklahoma is home to the second-largest Native American population in the United States, with Arizona and New Mexico following close behind. Many tourists come to the Southwest to take in the colorful **powwows** and festivals that celebrate the varied Native American culture.

(left) This cowboy is roping a steer at a roping competition in Llano, Texas.
(below) Over four million people from all around the world visit the Grand Canyon every year.

Timeline

17,000,000 B.C. – The Colorado river begins cutting the canyons of the Grand Canyon

1000 B.C. – The ancient Pueblo people, sometimes called the Anasazi, live in the Southwest region

1200 A.D. – Adobe houses and villages are built in canyons of present-day Arizona and New Mexico by Native American nations such as the Anasazi. Native Americans of the Apache nation move from present-day western Canada into the present-day Southwest region of the United States

1519 – Spanish explorer, Alonso Álvarez de Pineda, discovers Texas while searching for a water route from the Gulf of Mexico to Asia

1540-42 –Spanish explorer, Coronado, explores the Southwest region

1718 – San Antonio, Texas, is founded and becomes the center for Spanish missions in the Southwest

1821 – Mexico wins Mexican War of Independence from Spain. Spain no longer owns present-day Southwest region of United States

1822 – Stephen F. Austin becomes first empresario of Texas when he settles first Americans near the Brazos River

1836 – Texas claims independence from Mexico

1845 – Texas becomes 28th state in America

1889 – Oklahoma Land Run brings 50,000 settlers to the area in one afternoon

1936– Hoover Dam is built on the border of Arizona and Nevada

Find Out More

BOOKS

The Southwest (Regions of the United States) by Mark Stewart, Heinemann-Raintree, 2006.

The United States Region by Region by Patricia Kummer. Steck-Vaughn, 2002.

Exploring the Southwestern United States by Corinne J. Naden. Raintree, 2003.

WEBSITES

Discover more about the four states that make up the Southwest region at:
www.netstate.com

Learn everything you need to know about America's 50 states at:
www.50states.com

Follow along with explorers as they uncover facts and history about the states that make up the Four Corners at:
www.questconnect.org/sw_american_southwest.htm

Glossary

adobe A sun-dried brick of mud or clay

annex To add or attach

cattle drive To move a herd of cows from one location to another

continent One of seven large landmasses on Earth

empresario A land agent who managed land grants and American settlers when Spain or Mexico owned much of the Southwest region

groundwater Water that is found beneath the ground

Hispanic People of Spanish heritage

humid Having a high amount of water or moisture in the air

hydroelectric Producing electricity using waterpower

migrate To move from one region or country to another

nomadic Moving often from one place to another

plateau A raised landform or area that is higher than surrounding areas

powwow A Native American social gathering that often includes music and dance

replenish To fill up again

reservation An area of land set aside for Native Americans

Index